HORSELIFE

Published by Willow Creek Press, Inc.
P.O. Box 147, Minocqua, Wisconsin 54548

Photographs © the following contributors

p6 © Ron Kimball/www.kimballstock.com; p11 © Konrad Wothe/Minden Pictures; p12-13 © Konrad Wothe/Minden Pictures; p14 © Marios Liogris/500px; p16-17 © Juan Manuel Valle/agefotostock.com; p19 © Slawik.com; p20 © Slawik.com; p23 © Julia Shepeleva/500px; p25-25 © Slawik.com; p29 © Slawik.com; p30 © Yuxiao Chen/ricoh2000/500px; p33 © Daniel Sands/agefotostock.com; p37 © Slawik.com; p39 © Slawik.com; p40-41 © Barbara Neal/Getty Images; p42 © Roy McPeak/500px; p44 © James Ross/Stocksy.com; p45 © Ozana Sturgeon/500px; p47 © Klein and Hubert/Minden Pictures; p49 © Steve Smith/agefotostock.com; p50 © Klein-Hubert/www.kimballstock.com; p52 © Tony Đ/500px; p55 © Slawik.com; p56 © Kristel Richard/NPL/Minden Pictures; p58 © Richard Ligon/500px; p59 © Morales/agefotostock.com; p61 © Patricio Robles Gil/NPL/Minden Pictures; p62-63 © Pablo Dolsan/agefotostock.com; p64 © JUNIORS BILDARCHIV/agefotostock.com; p67 © Slawik.com; p70-71 © Dave and Les Jacobs/agefotostock.com; p73 © Slawik.com; p75 © Jim Brandenburg/Minden Pictures; p76 © Carey Dils/500px; p81 © Carey Dils/500px; p82 © Carol Walker/NPL/Minden Pictures; p85 © Klein-Hubert/www.kimballstock.com; p86 © AUSLOOS Henry/agefotostock.com; p89 © Jeremy Woodhouse/Holly Wilmeth/agefotostock.com; p94 © Slawik.com; p96 © Bernard Castelein/NPL/Minden Pictures; p97 © robertharding/Masterfile; p98 © Jonathan Lhoir/Biosphoto/Minden Pictures; p102 © Konstantin Tronin/500px; p105 © Kevin Russ/Stocksy.com; p106 © Mark J. Barrett/www.kimballstock.com; p109 © Yva Momatiuk and John Eastcott/Minden Pictures; p110-111 © Slawik.com; p114 © Carey Dils/500px; p115 © Thomas CAMUS/agefotostock.com; p117 © Polina Lurie/agefotostock.com; p118 © Wendy Kennedy/agefotostock.com; p121 © Slawik.com; p122 © Riley J.B./Stocksy.com; p124-125 © Michael Wheatley/agefotostock.com; 127 © Slawik.com; p128 © Slawik.com; p130 © Hans Zitzler/500px; p132-133 © Slawik.com; p138-139 © Slawik.com; p141 © Slawik.com; p141 © GIG/Stocksy.com;

Printed in China

HORSELIFE

RIDE SOFTLY, LISTEN CAREFULLY & LOVE COMPLETELY

WILLOW CREEK PRESS®

set your

heartbeat

to hoofbeats

feel the wind in

your hair

and the sun on your face

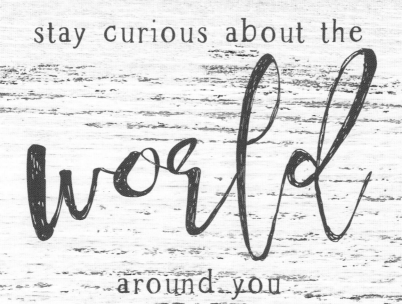

stay curious about the world around you

you have
one life
live it

kick up your *heels*

cherish

your independence

make new

friends

reconnect with *old ones*

savor quiet

moments

together

tell someone
how much you
care

better yet

show

them

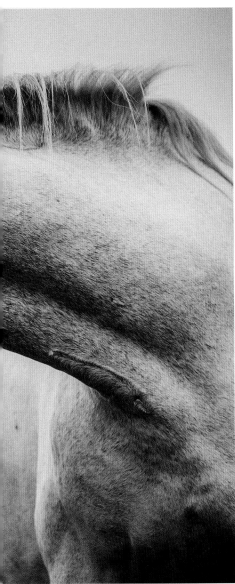

run with the *herd* but think for yourself

work as a *team* to reach your goals

the most

valuable

thing you'll ever earn is trust

blaze new trails

take the road less

traveled

don't let

obstacles

stand in your way

find your

mountain

to climb

take time to enjoy the

view

always

remember

where you came from

take the

long way

home

you'll go
farther with

the wind

at your back

get back to the

basics

drink plenty of

water

stretch

out of your comfort zone

learn to walk

before

you gallop

scratch what *itches*

a smile is the easiest way to improve your appearance

be proud

of your accomplishments

stand

out in a crowd

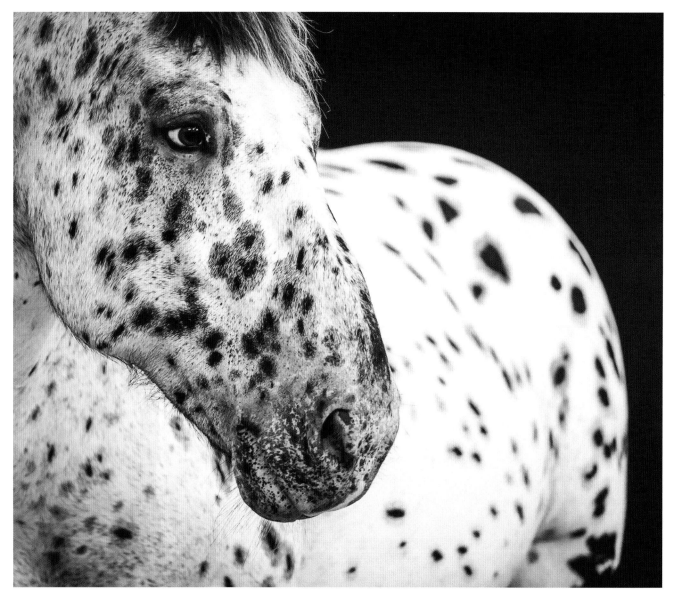

stay

humble

give somebody a lift

sometimes a *nudge* is all they need

be

accepting

it takes *strength* to be gentle

treasure **advice** from those that have been there

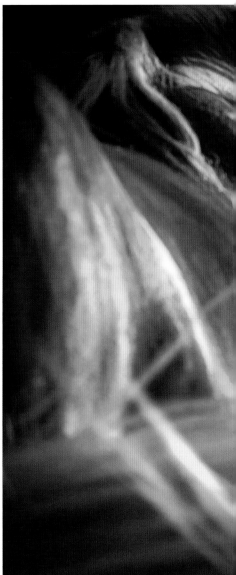

if you're

it will show in your eyes

stand up
for what you
believe in

don't

back down

there is *always sun* above the clouds

the grass is not always

greener

on the other side

take time to *smell* the flowers

life has its

majestic

moments

race with your

feet

not with your

mind

find

peace

in your breath

tend to your soul

nurture

your spirit